The American Gun

a poem by

Jessica Femiani

Finishing Line Press
Georgetown, Kentucky

The American Gun

Publisher: Leah Huete de Maines
Editor: Christen Kincaid
Cover Art: A *Good Shot, the Adirondacks* by Winslow Homer
Author Photo: Antonio D'Alfonso
Cover Design: Elizabeth Maines McCleavy

Order online: www.finishinglinepress.com
also available on amazon.com

Author inquiries and mail orders:
Finishing Line Press
PO Box 1626
Georgetown, Kentucky 40324
USA

I dedicate this poem to the memory of my maternal grandfather Antonio Pica (1915-2003), and his daughter, my mother, Kathleen Pica Femiani, for their tremendous hearts, love of story, and dedication to family.

I.

My great-grandfather was born a serf on land barren.

His wife, my great-grandmother, she said the land was cursed.

The riches of the waters reserved for the sons of families noble.

I know the story about a boy, Antonio, my grandfather.

One day he reached high above a wood-burning stove.

The muscles of his left arm stretched long and lean.

Just as his fingertips grazed the shells of hard-boiled eggs
stowed high.

His right elbow dipped, submerged, the water rolled a fast boil.

For the rest of his life, the skin of my grandfather's elbow
showed a pale pink, a glossed chap.

II.

My grandfather was a plumber, a foreman, a Democrat, a proud
      union man.

Built like a bull, he hauled cast-iron tubs up flights of stairs.

When my mother divides his wares, we each receive a mini
      leather-bound booklet,

pages full of rust-red stamps, stamped "dues paid," in rows,
      gathered in groups of four.

My mother, she remembers the NRA leaflets would arrive in the
      mail each month,

pages devoted to the pursuit, the chase that is sport.

The hunter pumps the rifle, pumps bullets to the chamber,
    shoots the deer fair game.

My grandmother, she cooked it all—venison to squirrel stew.

I can still hear my grandfather as he licks his lips, sucks the
    bones dry.

III.

I stand on the platform at 103rd Street & Corona Plaza, and I
   want the school day gone.

I fall in love with ugly and old, the textured peel of old bricks
   gessoed white, the fade of ads, factories, services, all
   past due.

Here on this platform, the billboards boast scenes of the
   summer's blockbuster hopefuls, all woven in threads of
   iron and steel.

I think of this amendment, penned to arm pioneers in the
   wilderness, militiamen, they'd band together on foot.

And I think about the middle school boys I teach, the crumpled
   papers I find in the garbage, shoved in their desks.

The finest jet-black inked line drawings, drawn as delicate and
elegant as lace.

Hatched lines ennoble a masculine zeal for a mysterious skin,
gunmetal cold, black, blue.

IV.

On the drive to Wegman's, I groove to Dar Williams,

Southern California wants to be Western New York.

At the red, my eyes land on the truck just ahead, the dark tint of
    its back window contrasts.

The white stenciled silhouette of a semiautomatic.

Below in clean white cursive reads, Come and get it!

A slight chill curls the warm autumn air.

I follow the truck as it parks, watch the driver, this tall man—
    with his legs long, his strides strong.

Watch as he shops, bags apples, picks out a few pears.

Watch as he glances at the list in his back pocket.

I can't help but notice the complete calm of his reserve,

the thin of his lips, without the subtlety of a curve, just dense
reddish-golden hair crowding his mouth.

V.

On the sunniest of December afternoons in Corona, Queens, I'm
    walking towards the 7 train on National Street.

Like always, I walk past a Buddhist temple, and it is likely a fat
    stub of incense is burning pine in a well of sand.

I can't remember details like that now, kind of how I can't
    remember if all the shoes were laid outside of the
    mosque that I pass next, the mosque I believe is the
    same mosque I once read Malcolm X founded.

Past a commercial laundry, a bodega, the Jehovah's Witness's
    Hall, all the places I know.

The taquerias, the Columbian bakery where I buy homemade
    hot sauce.

On this fourteenth of December, I hardly take notice, I'm
    sweating too much.

Having thrown my jacket over my shoulder, on the phone with
    my mother, we're talking, trying to piece together what
    happened.

I can still hear the high-pitched squawking of the crows high in the treetops as my mother tells me,

This young man, this young man's surname is a beautiful Italian name.

Like a famous opera singer my grandmother once loved.

This young man, my mother tells me,

He shot eighteen first graders, execution style.

Sky blue walls

glazed pomegranate red

and molasses smears.

The next day I do the unthinkable, try to talk the untalkable, to the
        stares of blank that belong to the children who have
        been my students the last two and a half years.

I can see their faces, complexions of rich cocoa butters, golden
        honey, jet streams of thick black hair, dark brown eyes
        searching.

They don't talk today during the announcements, even as our
        principal announces all that we already know.

A moment of silence is had, and he says, *The entire staff of I.S.
        61 and all its students will be keeping the students and
        teachers of Sandy Hook in our hearts and our prayers.
        But, we must all remain vigilant. Do not open any doors,
        for anyone under any circumstance.*

Ramon asks me, *What if we clean out the storage closet in the
        back, make it into a fort? A hideout for our class?*

Stock it with phone chargers, bottles of water, snacks?

The voice on the intercom drills *Soft Lockdown, Hard Lockdown.*

Those already locked classroom doors, standing open at the
    ready, slam them shut, hit the lights.

Cram kids into coat closets, under desks, away from the
    windows.

Count rosters.

That child crying out in the hall.

                        Leave that child behind.

VI.

The year I graduated high school when fire drills were nothing
    more than a break from class

the world birthed a boy, given the middle name of Storm.

As a child, he was said to stand apart, staring for hours at the
    flat of bedroom walls.

Happy he was, to talk casual of his dreams to kill.

Swayed by Emmanual African Methodist Episcopal Church's
    easy entrance, its evening bible study underway.

This young man found Black parishoners, young and old, sitting
    round with eyes closed, hands folded in prayer.

The lead preacher, a young senator, my age, married with two
    baby girls, pulls out a chair in welcome.

An invitation for this young man to close his eyes, fold his
    hands in prayer.

The warmth, the kindness of the parishioners almost convinced this young man to abort.

This young man believed Black men were taking over the country.

That Black men were raping white women.

Not having ever learned that Black men have never made rape a practice as our Founding Fathers did.

The rape of Black enslaved women.

This young man's moves were fortified in cyberspace.

He chose eighty-eight bullets, eighty-eight hollow-point bullets.

Designed to expand catastrophically, exponentially within the
body's tissues.

VII.

In the next time of too many, the shooter clanged bells, blew
    whistles, honked all the horns, squashed the squeaky
    wheel.

This young man chose Saint Valentine's as the day of all days to
    pump lead at school.

Stoneman Douglas has been left seventeen down.

They should what happens when kids are taught smart, how the
    young can see straight.

They stand up, they call foul, they keep the call-to-foul on a
    world of men consumed by pockets thick.

These men old, they don't think to heed the ways of a woman
    wise.

Maybe they hadn't heard of New Zealand?

After two mosques in Christchurch are gunned down, fifty-one
    Muslims slaughtered mid-prayer.

The Prime Minister of New Zealand, Jacinda Arden, she
    wraps her arms around the people.

Leads a parliament divided to negotiate, then legislate a
    ban on the country's military-style weapons.

All assault rifles, its semiautomatic rifles, the high-capacity
    magazines, all banned.

VIII.

This time, the shooter posts a manifesto of hate directed at our
    brethren, Black and brown.

Before driving forty-eight hours cross-state, ramming his fearless
    heart of hate amidst aisles of a Walmart in El Paso.

For the love of God, wasn't Texas stolen from Mexico, anywho?

This time of next, the shooter brings vengeance underground
    rich red splatters off subway tile in South Brooklyn,
    my sister marks herself safe.

This time, every time of too many, young White men rage.

We cannot comprehend the slaughter, we cannot make
    meaning of this magnitude.

We do what people do, we enact life's doing, the cooking, the
    cleaning, the loving, the working, the schooling.

The supermarket, a shopping mall, an elementary school, a
    movie theater, the mall again, another mall, a nightclub,

a college dormitory, high schools, grade schools, this
parade, that concert, this state, that state, every state,

three shootings in the same state, the same week, ten
dead, twelve dead, twenty-five.

We want to put our baby to sleep, five dead.

The man said, if he'd known he wouldn't have sold him the gun.

IX.

What is to be said if men salaried, with guns, gear, and
protections massive, if they too, are afraid?

If they stand outside Robb Elementary fumbling over the chain
of command while the shooter shoots the babies inside?

The parents in Uvalde had no bodies to claim, a cotton swab to
the cheek identifies their remains.

I spend most of my time in my apartment these days.

If I decide to run out for a carton of milk, I worry this could be a
bad time. Might this be the same time, another young
man in America decides to make his descent?

If this is my adult mind, I can't begin to imagine the dreams of
the children asleep in their beds.

Bedtime prayers become urgent pleas.

Please God, please don't let me be killed at school. Please watch
over me when I am in church, playing at Mikey's house,
in the mosque, the synagogue.

Dreams that haunt, disrupt the sleep, baritone yells cut the
night.

X.

I have spent precious time worrying how I might bring this
poem to a close.

Even more worrying this helplessness will persist.

We've been in it for so long, walking backward.

What is a country that cannot protect its people? It's children?

What then is the future? How is this freedom, America?

For the longest, I've not known where to look, but my eyes now
fall on the shoulders of the youth.

The young people drilling since they were born.

Having watched classmates and friends and teachers dying in
pools of blood in classrooms and cafeterias across this
land.

The young adults, they've got it, they've got verve.

In the high heat of summer, they took to the streets in hordes.

Their legs traversing the nation, chanting beneath masks, masks masking breath, chanting *Black Life Matters.*

With voices hoarse and throats sore, chanting *No Justice, No Peace,* chanting still, *Into the Streets.*

Chanting and marching for this life, our life, our lives.

Chanting for the living and breathing, a revolution of being.

ACKNOWLEDGMENTS

First and foremost, I'd like to acknowledge Leah Huete de Maines, publisher of Finishing Line Press, who selected this manuscript for publication. I am very grateful that she is helping this poem make its way into the world. I would also like to thank my editor, Christen Kincaid, and the entire team at Finishing Line Press.

I would like to express my sincere gratitude to the very fine poets, Jim Daniels, Cammy Pedroja, and Melissa Tuckey, who read this manuscript and wrote kind and generous blurbs.

Additionally, I am grateful to Binghamton University's writing community. I am indebted to my advisor, Joe Weil, for his support and guidance, particularly his impeccably sharp and generous ear. I would very much like to acknowledge the guiding hand that Tina Chang gently offered. It was she who selected this poem from my dissertation manuscript, *At the Foot of a Volcano*, encouraging its revival after it had long been buried.

I would like to pay homage to J. Barret Wolf and Kayla Volpe, the tireless and magnanimous hosts of the weekly Thursday Night Poetry series at the Belmar, in Binghamton, NY, where much of this poem was brought to life during the before times. Thank you for creating a most welcoming and warm creative space and encouraging artistic growth and expression. I am immensely grateful to Jefferson and Nicholas Taze Yanick for pushing me through.

A special thank you to the many poets with whom I workshopped excerpts of this poem via Zoom: in particular, Shatha Almutawa, Iris Marie Bloom, Fran Markover, Jaime Lee Jarvis, Catherine Johnson, Gretchen Herman, Barbara Pease, and Mary Jane Richmond.

With a wonderfully full heart, I thank my entire family, all who have gathered round, especially my parents, Kathleen, and Ralph Femiani, who believed in my love for poetry.

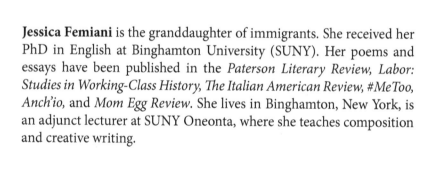

Jessica Femiani is the granddaughter of immigrants. She received her PhD in English at Binghamton University (SUNY). Her poems and essays have been published in the *Paterson Literary Review, Labor: Studies in Working-Class History, The Italian American Review, #MeToo, Anch'io,* and *Mom Egg Review.* She lives in Binghamton, New York, is an adjunct lecturer at SUNY Oneonta, where she teaches composition and creative writing.

Printed in the USA
CPSIA information can be obtained
at www.ICGtesting.com
CBHW022154170824
13359CB00009B/548